# Wild Persistence

A mí se me hace cuento que existiera un lugar al que pertenecer, un árbol sin raíces' – *Andrés Neuman.*

Hard to believe there might exist a place to belong, a tree without roots – *Andrés Neuman* (translated by Richard Gwyn).

# Wild Persistence

*Katrina Naomi*

Seren is the book imprint of
Poetry Wales Press Ltd.
57 Nolton Street, Bridgend, Wales, CF31 3AE
www.serenbooks.com
facebook.com/SerenBooks
twitter@SerenBooks

ISBN: 978-1-78172-581-8
ebook: 978-1-78172-582-5

A CIP record for this title is available from the British Library.

The publisher acknowledges the financial assistance of the Welsh Books Council.

Cover photograph: 'Martha Graham – Celebration (trio)' 1937 by Barbara Morgan.

Author photograph: Tim Ridley.

Author website: www.katrinanaomi.co.uk

Author twitter: @KatrinaNaomi

Printed in Bembo by Severn, Gloucester.

# Contents

# Anti-
## ambient

A joy of noise
like a whole fucking Motörhead
splitting the monochrome
sparking a choice
of dark or light
a crossing     revelling
in a migraine
of sound

The shadow
self asserts
stepping out
of the gunsmoke
ignoring the safety of grey

There are different ways to live

# London: A Reply

A year on and I can't hear you.
You have left me, dear London,
like I left you. I could drop this tiff,
walk the seven minutes to your big white bus,
climb aboard. I know you've tried,
you've sent me images through the ether: Soho
early morning, Hyde Park in the sun,
Charing Cross Road's bookshops
before the chain of dull cafés,
but in this reaching out, you've made yourself
so much quieter, perhaps in the way
two people mirror each other,
adjusting the tilt of their heads,
how they move their arms, take on accents.

Yours is a kind of wooing, dear London,
and while I cried and cried at leaving you,
you'd taken on airs, become grandiose
with the possibilities of capital. And I saw
something new, somewhere I'd visited
long ago on a rainy night, playing pool
in a pub near a seaside bus station.
Had I lost the game that night, perhaps
I'd never have come here –
that's how decisions are made. I'm sorry,
dear London, it's over. But you'll go on
reinventing yourself, building taller,
as if you could see me from one of your towers.

# How to Celebrate a Birthday

Turn off your computer, you're not at work
today. There will be drink and food and friends.
There may or may not be cake. You'll also want,
as well as presents and good sex, a little time alone.
Not to look back but to think about who you are.
A year is immaterial but it's what we understand;
a better time than New Year to think of who you are,
what you love and what you might change.
It's important to feel a little bit special,
even before the cava. And there has to be cava.
You can let go of any worry – like the string of a balloon
that may or may not have a number of years frosted
against the pink. Let it go, let the years go,
let who you'd hoped you'd be by now go. Celebrate
who you are. Put up your cards, display your gifts,
though the vegan fudge needs to sit in the fridge,
it can cosy up to what's left of the cava. Smile
at whoever you meet. Swim in the sea, with or without
friends, consider how each wave greets you. Dance
to your favourite Sister Sledge, the neighbours
shouldn't mind too much, for it's your birthday.
Allow yourself to be treated for lunch, then walk
home across the moor, making time for a snooze
in the sun – inevitable after all the cava. Make love
before you go out tonight – you'll become
more beautiful, this is what people say. And,
if you can – and you can – dance some more.
Dancing shows us who we really are
and who we might become. Go on, dance.
And look up at the stars on your way
back, look at them for longer than usual.
Find one that might burn for you; name it.

# At Noongallas

*for Kenza*

A brooding sky,
cows stumbling down a hill.
So much life and death on a farm.
And out of this huge dampness, a thin cry
like a mewling kitten or a tropical bird –
part West Cornwall, part West Africa –
something undefinable.
We spoke of you last night
having no name for you then.
As we talked, a meteor shower, an omen
short-lived but powerful. And your father said:
*At home, we believe the stars burst*
*into the atmosphere before falling to the sea.*
We felt we were taken somewhere else –
a campsite, beers, talk in English and French –
and that belly still, silent, waiting
to be heard across the sodden fields,
your mother's waters having run all night.

Your mother's waters having run all night
to be heard across the sodden fields
and that belly still, silent, waiting.
A campsite, beers, talk in English and French.
We felt we were taken somewhere else –
into the atmosphere before falling to the sea.
At home, we believe the stars burst –
short-lived but powerful. And your father said,
as we talked, *a meteor shower – an omen –*
having no name for you. Then
we spoke of you last night:
something undefinable,
part West Cornwall, part West Africa,
like a mewling kitten or a tropical bird.
And out of this huge dampness, a thin cry –
so much life and death on a farm,
cows stumbling down a hill,
a brooding sky.

# Swaling on Boscathow

*for David May*

The farmer tosses purple moor grass into the air –
*An Easterly* – we're ready to burn.
Pale grey puffs become a bonfire guy legging it
through gorse and bracken. The fire doesn't burn
into the ground, is all surface and speed.
I'm responsible for my patch but if the wind were to run
away, I'd sprint this grassy corridor
or be sacrificed to some god I've yet to hear of.

Annie asks me what to do
as if I've worked a fire this size before.
The contractor, who set the fire,
would be handsome on a film set. Here,
he's in frayed red T-shirt, hole-ridden overalls
open to the groin. I like that he says *he*
instead of the English–English *him* –
*I've worked with he before.*

The fire finds its own voice, stalls,
worries at a tussock before lurching on.
A shrew bolts. The fire leaves
part of itself, teasy as an orange baby,
writhing by my boots. I do my job and whack it.
The farmer nods – *almost done.*
We breathe in the distant danger,
paraffin rides the air.

# Bardhonek May Hwisk Hi Ynno Hy Fows Dhemmedhyans Meurgerys

hag yw kesunyans a vor hag a ydhyn.
Yma syns oll a-dro dhedhi. Hern ha brithel
a dernij a-dhiworth roesow ewynek hy goelesennow.
Ha hi ow tevera, yma lies cher dhe'n bows –
moy es pali, moy es owrlin.
Pows kryghys yw, pows may neuvir ynni,
pows hag ynni re erel a bys. Pows yw
a neb bri, pows a dhirol
der hy diwvregh, a gudh hag a dhiskudh hy fenn.
Ha tergh an mordid ow kildenna, paloresow a fast aga neyth
yn hy gols gwynsek, aga diwarr dhergh ha'ga gelvin
owth afina. Homm yw pows rag karjel ha fyll.
Homm yw pows rag hager-awel – pows owrek ha gwynn,
ha glas ha rudh, ha du. Y'n bows ma,
hi a omglew hanter-Kristones, ow krysi
y'n henwyn koth – an re kerys,
an re kellys – Alef, Cadoc, Dungarth, Salomon.
Ha'n debron erbynn hy kroghen, hi a as
dhe goedha an gwias, ow tos ha bos henhwedhel. Tirwel.

*Translated into Cornish from Katrina's English-language
original by Katrina Naomi and Steve Penhaligon*

## Poem in Which She Wears Her Favourite Wedding Dress

which is a marriage of sea and birds.
Saints are all about her. Herring and mackerel
flit from the frothing nets of underskirts.
As it drips, the dress has many moods –
more than velvet, more than silk.
It is a ruffled dress, a dress in which to swim,
a dress in which others pray. It is a dress
of some import, a dress which reels
through her arms, covers and uncovers her head.
As the tidal collars retreat, choughs fix their nests
in her windy hair, their bright legs and beaks
ornament. This is a dress for accordions and fiddles.
This is a dress for a storm – a dress of gold and white,
and blue and red, and black. In this dress,
she senses she is half-Christian, believes
in the old names – those she loved,
those she lost – Alef, Cadoc, Dungarth, Salomon.
With the itch against her skin, she lets
the fabric fall, becomes mythology. Landscape.

# Maybe Owls

*for John Searles*

The birds in the silver birches listened
as we shone our light over rock
jutting through the moss and grass
of the path. The night silenced us,
we became aware of the still sky
and the stars we were ignorant of.
The need for concentration was there
for the cliff fell away to our left.
At the bend in the path, the birds
took their chance – screeched and flapped
at us, as if we were intruders,
as if we had no right to the dark.
You grasped my arm, my hair,
as you forced my arm over your shoulder
and cowered – an awkward half-kneel,
the torch beam making an involuntary cross
against the woods. I've never known a man
make me hug him. For an instant
I considered if this was all a pretence –
your ornithophobia – but the birds
must have been pleased at their work
for you opened your mouth and screamed,
almost an enjoyment in the pitch of it.
And again – that release.
I used my in-control voice, steady
and stern, which also came
of its own volition. I heard my words,
considered them and our many selves,
considered again the shelter you took
and how the stars didn't recognise us either,
and the night went on, knowingly.
Under my command, we walked back,
faster than we'd come. And you let my arm go.
Stood apart. And I thought, later, maybe owls,
with their whiteness, their bright moon faces,
and how quickly the quiet folded the sounds
away, blending them into the dark, the night
mending itself, the sounds carried
by the river and away down the valley.

# Dualism: A Manifesto

*for Jesse Leroy Smith*

Think what I could achieve by          splitting myself

One hand
one side of the brain to write or paint          the other to perform
                                                  the mundane jobs
                                                  that persist in
                                                  winking at me
God got greedy
choosing to be three people          Let's have no truck with that

At once I could be
the one who vogues to Eurovision
in orange sequinned stiletto          and the other who reads
                                      yet another Iris Murdoch
                                      in cream and brown brogue

Monocles would be fashionable          hopping essential

I could allow
the male and female personae
their freedom
could be half buzzcut          half quiff
                               So could you

I've yet to decide if the two
would rejoin at night          or if like a pair of Tories
                               we'd squabble in separate beds
                               pushed far against each wall
                               each eye shut and turned
                               from the other

I could belt out Shirley Bassey          and air guitar
                                          'Bring Your Daughter
                                          to the Slaughter'
                                          with some difficulty

eat vegan sushi
in a revolving restaurant in Tokyo      and Mother's Pride
sugar sarnies
in a Margate council house


I could sup London Pride      and knock back two
jugloads of gin
Cornish of course


One part of me could flip through
shit magazines by a Magaluf pool      while the other does something
far too energetic
to describe here


I would learn to fall      with dignity


could even go as far
as to consider a problem      from both sides


There's the question
of which of the selves would retain
our genitalia
otherwise sex would require
greater ingenuity      This might not be a bad thing


Different coloured socks
would be the norm


One side of me could be utterly lovable      The other
who I really am

# Elemental

I shouldn't have lied when you asked about the mud.
Had I told you I press a cleat from the boots of the men
who walk up from the village, you might have found this odd.
While they sleep, I bend each sole until a wedge of packed earth
falls onto my palm. Something from the outside, coming in.

Had you pulled the curtain, you'd have seen a jar
of my nan's hair, woollen in its whiteness.
I used to free the wisps from the comb's tines with forefinger
and thumb; poke out with a pin the dark of the gunk and grease.
Had you asked, you might have found this strange.

And had you moved the jar, looked, further back,
you'd have seen a tin of glass and small, sharp stones
gouged from the tyres of my dad's Austin Traveller.
Like an occupation, just something I did, sat on the kerb,
cradling rubber; my very first touch of a screwdriver.

You can shake the tin, it's all there. I'm more selective,
now, in my choice of chevrons, zig-zags and tubes of soil.
I don't clean their boots, that would admit a form of love,
but lay each treasure in a Perspex dish, something elemental,
and, you might say, bordering on the forensic.

# Interpretation

*With thanks to Yamanashi Prefectural Library*

I've almost stopped interpreting
yen – all those noughts.
I thought, at first, those notes haven't helped me
write a poem. I recalled a man on Waterloo Bridge
who wrote poems for cash. I offered £2,
received a poem about love on orange paper,
a purple envelope. I could have paid £20, £20,000.
What could a poem be worth and to whom?
How many noughts should I add,
for a favourite poem? And how could it be owned,
no matter how many yen or pounds
in a shiny gold purse? None of these
philosophers in their remarkable robes
can buy such words. A poem's worth
everything and nothing. Perhaps
some of my philosophers understand. And yes,
it has cost me to sit in silence
in this spacious, air-conditioned place,
the philosophers asleep in the close confines
of their dreams. What would Austen say
on the matter? And if I threw these notes,
these dreaming philosophers, from the top
of this building, with its roofline trees,
typhoonish-blue sky, who's to say –
from such a distance – what is money,
who is royalty, what are mere jottings,
and which is a love poem written to a stranger?

*Yukichi Fukuzawa (1835–1901), a philosopher, writer and cultural critic, is one of the founders of modern Japan. His likeness appears on the 10,000 yen banknote.*

# Open Letter

*translated from Yohanna Jaramillo's original*

If you knew you went inside me after ten at night,
and were the reason for the spliff at 4.20 in the morning,
and something extra, like the expected email,
the call
            which is always answered.
If you knew that each verse I write
I re-read, in delay mode, for you;
I know how to manage brainwaves,
I know about metals and energy,
I know about carbon and my antenna-hair,
I know that fire and vegetables gather,
I know the secret of broccoli:
*It wants to be the drag queen of vegetables.*
I know that the only thing that doesn't grow with heat and water
is time,
that's why the sun is ecstatic,
that's why this planet is worried.
I know that all the masses which float
belong to us, we belong to them, we belong to each other.
And we spin,
and our rushing spins,
you don't catch up and we spin,
I write the truth and we spin.

The chemical elements of our bones,
the quarks, make us rotate
and we spin,
without vomiting, we spin,
a slow-motion turn,
the spinning top of 'someone' who explodes with the launch's speed,
*at top speed, the particles fall apart,*
and they said 'another turn and we go', and they went and left us, spinning.
*If you knew,* I say, like the @ncient poet,
as if modern verbs didn't exist
when we speak of love,
of this rare creation of society,
which is addictive.
That's why I write this with a dropper,

19

I'm a slow learner,
I'm accused of lacking ethics,
in this investigation.

# Mentor

*for Marisa Foz del Barrio*

You divorced on the first day
it was legal, were imprisoned
three times as a Communist
under Franco, still dyed your hair
blonde and – at the age I am now –
still lived with your parents'
bourgeois furniture (those impossible beds),
the drapes and porcelain from another era,
one you'd rebelled against
but kept close by, as if to understand
yourself better. I think of you
sitting under your father's army awards,
a carpet-style brocade over the table
and over your knees, a lamp
at your feet, like an old woman,
your rollie constantly giving up
in the green ash tray. And me,
curled on the stiff sofa, trying
to follow your every word –
for you never spoke in English,
never explained. You took me in,
gave me a key, smiled when I climbed
to your flat roof in a bikini in January,
shared bread and manchego
when my grant was late.
I last saw you a decade back,
you looked much the same,
smoked much the same.
I wish we still spoke on the phone,
because one day I'll press the buzzer
to your flat and you won't be in.

# Spared

I have found seven hearts
       lost one    found six more   They hang
like Xmas decs on a wedding tree so much bad
       wallpaper    And I'm unsure
if I'm indoors   or out
       The trellis shifts
for some unseen bird that comes
       like a suitor
not one you'll welcome
       if you know what I know
A normal asylum then this
       a century of roses and killer-birds
all too ready to tip breathing hearts
       from the nest   for these are the rules
of marriage   Such a common
       selective    madness
wisdom    caught on a white rose briar   So brittle
       this pale domesticity   I could snap
your wishbone   White crowds
       a room    walls unable to march
back or forth    And so many choose this space
       where all ties are
severed for the ice and snow
       of love    its crazed pattern
of fracture and fall
       Every girl's dream
for a veil   to render her beautiful
       as we fail
to look a suitor in the face
       for we have been sold   Nothing
here is straight   We see shadows
       of ourselves    the door slowly barred
with so much love    There is no such thing
       as claustrophobia    Trust me
I am perfectly safe here    can only hear
       one bird   the killer-bird
out of season    its suitor voice plays
       to all the seasons of my life

an extreme bird     a favourite
      yet you will not find her
among the neon lights of sky
      for I am one to have been
spared

# After the Shock of your Photo on Facebook

or what someone had tagged as you, running on a farm track
into a forest. A photo from a distance –

do I really know it's you? After a week, I hoped,
in some secret to myself, for a letter,

my name in your slanted hand under a Czech stamp
of a bird or a flower or an artist –

your touch, lasting all the way from the forest,
if it really was you?

And I would've held something
I thought I understood –

and maybe your lips would've said my name
as you wrote. Still,

I've been busy with books, a novel of magic, love
and the circus – mostly the circus –

and a book of poetry from another century,
as if I might force some emotion.

I can't seem to love like poets love. All I can say
is I find myself sat in the dark –

staring, as if I can make you out. I've unscrewed
the silver top of your aftershave,

closed my eyes. I want to taste the cherry vodka you may be drinking.
That photo, your face turned away –

will I know you at the station, with your half-remembered vowels,
your North Bohemian looks?

You will arrive, nine days from now,
with your new history –

I will put down my books. I don't know if I'll tell you
how long a day can be; an evening even longer.

# On Fucking

*after Roddy Lumsden*

There's that word to straddle, the idea
that this act, or series of acts –
to be precise – could count
as swearing, though it's sometimes a whisper,
sometimes a shout, sometimes a noise
we've never known before. And this is private
swearing; we're not ones to go public
or exhibit ourselves, for this can be over-
rather than X-rated; but when it's good,
it's very good. We have gone for days –
a week, or two has been known –
and the inevitability is palpable,
why haven't we done this
to ourselves? We find each other
again, away from all that business
of making a life and try not to laugh
at the squelch and play of us, the scrabble
and too many limbs, loving
that journey from the bed, floor
or field to someplace further
with its own smell and sound,
its lights going off and on, and we don't
smoke, though we've a need for
something after – the shared taste
and remembrance – until the next time
when we've shifted too far
from each other. Fucking
is neither sacred nor profane;
we're not interested in the survival
of the species, just each other,
this person behind the clothes
and skin, this honest enjoyment
and need, with its element of should;
for we are lazier than we think;
then we'll glimpse the other side
of each other, somewhere inappropriate
and we know. And this, this fucking
is ours; then there can be no telling.

# On Suitors

Emily Dickinson had the right idea
speaking with her suitors through a door
seeking to be swayed not by gifts or looks
but by the qualities of a voice –
what a person has to say, the essence
of intonation, distilled with wit and intelligence.
To listen, to listen only, and imagine
the kind of man or woman
outside. And I think of Skype, the similarities
of talking without pixilation's dull entreaties
to see and be seen. I am freeing
myself in this lovely prison of my making.
I prefer isolation. And when they come,
I stay in my room, leave them
at the foot of the stairs; I stay alone,
I'm not being rude but I choose to listen
to the syntax, the accent, the colour
of a voice, not to be wooed by a suitor,
how they choose to show
themselves, how they modify or allow
their words to be uttered, whether they are found
worth listening to, whether they listen in return.
There are those who've tried thrusting
photos under doors, onto screens. The good looking
I won't tolerate, let alone the rest. I do not discriminate.
I'll allow a suitor to ruminate –
briefly. I want to fall in love with a voice
and then – only then – decide on a face.
You're welcome to whisper at a keyhole,
to speak by the pale green wall.
Without mystery there can be no drunkenness
of love. And you may have guessed –
like Emily – I've no real interest in release.

# Beat

A former marathon runner, you're proud
of your heartbeat, so slow I can seldom find
your pulse. I'd like it to quicken, to know
that it quickens for me. I remember my mother
saying I had a good man – and not to lose him.
I asked what she meant. I'd never thought of you
leaving. Mum talked of my travels, study,
friendships: *There aren't many men like him,*
*you know.* I think of her words, when we're
apart, and worry just a little, then return
to my routine on the island, alone. I know you
found it hard, my climbing into the minibus,
being driven to the windswept airport.
I'd hugged you through your favourite suit,
watched you turn the corner, imagined you
walking up the hill, deciding which lane
to choose back to our house, and recalled
you joking, as you often do: *You will come back?*
After you'd gone, I texted 'I love you',
didn't wait for a reply, pressed the Nokia's side,
silenced my messages for the week.
My mother's voice is older, can't be turned off.
I console myself with you saying,
as I lay on your chest three days ago,
when we last made love, how you could feel
my heart beating. It's still so much faster
than yours. You, who are happy
to stay in one place, who's slowed down,
who knows he has all he wants or needs.

# What Arrival Feels Like

Tugging the cold window down
I check myself, worried
I'll feel shy or regretful in some way, unsure
if the tears are caused by the rush of night
air, the thought of you, or the lights of Penzance –
their gaudy echo in the bay – or just my eyes' blur
after no sleep for 36 hours. The time has gone
backwards and forwards. I saw two sunsets
on an 11-hour flight – can that be possible?
I focus, as best I can, on the moon, the stars,
the end of the land, knowing I can travel
no further.
                    I make believe I can see you,
way along the platform. After all these weeks,
I can. It's you in your green coat from Berlin,
I see your black jeans and zebra-print shoes,
a bunch of anemones in your left hand; your right
reaches mine as I lean from the train.
You hug me as I spill from the journey.
Our mouths touch, we say nothing out loud.
Now, I step back, look at you
properly, my tears wet
on your cheek.
                    Our talk on the brief walk home
is of the airplane food, the shop that's shut down,
a politeness that comes of distance,
knowing we'll talk and talk over the next few hours,
days and months, and before morning, we'll be naked –
then time and the longing will stop,
not just in this act but the moving towards
each other, in understanding each other's lives
again. And I will learn to give up
the sadness, the joy and the normality
of having been alone –
and not be reluctant.

# How Is It

that a person in bed is not quite a person –
not until they have gained their height,
brushed the dark from their hair, wiped the weight
of granite from the edge of their eyes?
Standing, we become ourselves, vertebra by vertebra.
Some add messages to their eyelids and nails.
This can make the human harder to locate
as we recover from shutting the known out,
breathing it out in strange, strangled voices,
keeping lovers awake, watchful. We let the mouth
fall away from itself, allowing in new thoughts
to squirm through lower and upper tubes.
Something sacred in lying down, as if we are statues,
the cathedral kind, hands fixed, our bodies
blindly staring at less notable ceilings.
And we rise when a visitor enters, try to rearrange
our skin to its former gravity, wipe the drool
from our cheeks and smile. It's not just vulnerability –
that we may be naked under the duvet –
but the knowledge we could as easily crawl
from bed, return to a life on all fours.

# As if This were Someone Else's Drama

I forced myself awake
me and you so tired after waiting
five hours for the ambulance
We barely talked      I tried to stop
wiping my hands over my face
tried to read a wildlife magazine
badgers' young emerging about now
while you dozed      and when it was time
to wake up      that middle of the night dread
and excitement      bag packed as if
one of us was away for a holiday
a resolve that this was what we both wanted
And the paramedic's kindness
as she carried your bag      all those things
crammed in      It's like someone else
did that      thought of what you might need
dared to consider how many pairs of pants
how long the stay this time
The other paramedic called me *Lovely*
as I stood in the doorway      the whole street
flashing blue      and you stood so quiet
a sort of shuffle and slow climb
into that wheeled room      that other world
of 2.40 in the morning      You didn't
look back      I waited as if I might see you
wave goodbye      Of course you were lying
on your side      being prepared      I closed
the door      took the mugs to the kitchen
didn't clean my teeth      trod upstairs
with a hot water bottle to the sound of gulls

# Holidayish

I sit by the harbour in sun, a tourist drinking cappuccino
without a thought in her head, while you lay face down

as if for a massage; you've never been so relaxed, hypnotised
by the counting down. Once the magic's done,

they take their small knife and let themselves in. I thought I'd know
when they cut but there's nothing, not even an itch of blade.

I'm almost cheerful, while your lung is being incised,
scraped of its muck. I breathe deep, something to share with you

when you come round; then I'll hold my breath, hold
your hand, while you come back to me, back to yourself.

# You Told Yourself

you'd get up when you heard the owls,
you'd go out and find them high in the beeches
but you turned and reached for your partner's warm back.

Much later, you're alert to bird calls and watch,
while the kettle boils, for crow shapes, the flits
of wrens and robins. But you don't hear

an owl, no matter how long you sit by a rainy window. It's gone
8 o'clock. You told yourself, just last week,
while answering a questionnaire, that you'd no regrets.

# Ghazal for Tim

*Your body my fugitive forever* – Federico García Lorca

You'll always be in black Bauhaus T-shirt
The T-shirt's lost; our separate Bauhaus LPs sit together, forever

Our first date, Hyde Park, after college, on the swings
We were really that young; it's been forever

At the boat disco, I asked you to dance to Marvin Gaye
You'd already told a friend I'd be forever

I didn't know this, couldn't imagine
such a handsome, posh boy could be forever

Private school in Surrey, a Margate council estate
such different backgrounds stay with us forever

I knew it was serious when I travelled at nineteen
my restlessness must have seemed forever

You almost had an affair; I was also tempted
Neither of us has; blimey, forever

Even telling you I loved you – and meaning it –
was hard; hard to believe this could be forever

We've never mentioned this word, we're just
Katrina & Tim – no kids, marriage or joint account – just forever

# The University

You'll know the sort of place. The rooms
were large and purpose-built, yet lacked
beauty. There were trees, lots of courtyards –
I like this in a university, don't you?
But it wasn't a building I could love.
I tried to admire the form and function,
the ergonomics of it. But it lacked flamboyance,
any superfluous design. I like beauty –
have I said that before? I want more of it,
fewer straight lines, fewer courtyards with shale
or pebbles, and sensible dark green plants
with no flowers. Give me orange or pink
dahlias, give me blossom. Break
out of what passes for the mould of modernity.
I do not want to research in a grey-clad box.
I do not want to look up to an aluminium
balcony ever again. Give me windows
I can open. Forget the conditioning.
I'm sorry I didn't stay after
I'd been offered that post. I liked
the students, the lecturers, I just couldn't
put up with grey. I no longer felt myself.
But thank you, it was kind. And now
I feel hateful, and slightly ashamed.

# House as Tent

You walk uphill to sleep, downhill early morning –
and there's a flush – it's more complicated than slipping out,
squatting in the chill, the moon keeping its eye on you.
The back door hangs in the breeze, wanting to flap
like dark green nylon but lacking something. I miss the soft
bark of nesting magpies, we couldn't know we'd pitched
beneath them. I'll admit the bed's comfier here, without
the cold shriek of a mummy's zip. We were not as clean
as we might have been. I had a relationship
with fire. The pale blue box with its flue in the corner
is as nothing compared with the dry furze
gathered at the bright blue end of day, sparks
fleeing from the gorse and granite, stars watching
from their distance deciding whether to show themselves,
for there are almost no obligations on a moor.
Here, the big dipper just fits above our terrace,
it's a surprise I looked up at all. Here are many rooms;
there, just the two – indoors and out. Here, you wrestle
with a window, I had no window there; except for that space
when the moor's ponies and cattle stand, motionless
and you can think about the things that matter

# The Gift

On my way for a massage, I bumped across the moor
on the 10A, admired the first foxgloves, the tan bullock, the view
of the Isles of Scilly. Everything felt unexpected.
I found the house and Jude, giving life to plants
took off her gardening gloves, welcomed me to liquorice tea
on a Moroccan tray, like a giant sun. I was charmed there.
We took her favourite walk, *the dangerous route,*
a squeeze between rock, a ledge, that unforgiving scramble
above a feverish sea, to the thin safety of the coast path.
I chose ylang ylang, more floral than usual,
clambered onto the waist-high bed, fitted my face
to the spongy loop, my body beneath unseasonal blankets.
I came to as my legs were being finished. I'd been away
where I could see the flowers that had given
their bright lives so I could feel this good. Jude worked
the muscles of my neck, I couldn't prevent a grin,
and though it felt manipulated – given how ill you were –
I was glad of it, glad as she drove me back across the moor,
glad as I walked into our house, saw you,
standing, as if Jude had also, somehow, achieved this.

# The Table my Father Made

I'd always thought of my father as a carpenter –
Mum having spoken with pride of the table he'd made.
If nothing else survives of him, there's this 1960's
circle of teak, shining in our front room
with its blue hydrangeas, the table my partner and I
eat from. It's scored and stained with life's easy spillages.
I have nothing else from him, except some kink
of personality, his hair and eyes, a small photo of him
and Mum and me, when we were together.
As a teenager, keeping his table felt wrong,
but some part of Brazil had been spoilt
for this table's existence, for the sun to fall on it,
fracturing into long oblongs, for hydrangea seeds
to fall, as if to a forest floor. And I liked the styling
and the idea that my father – who I haven't seen
since I was seven – had crafted the wood,
shaped it into this circle, which could be taken down,
one flap at a time, made to fit a room,
how the teak lived on with his skill and care,
even if he didn't have these qualities in abundance.
I also spoke proudly of the table, preserved it
with an eco-friendly lavender polish,
when I remembered. My partner told me,
one night, that the table was assembled from a kit,
a forerunner to IKEA. And yes, this figures,
in the way my father always said he was a doctor;
I found out he was a nurse. He was never
a doctor, never a carpenter, never dedicated himself
to one woman or one family. But this table
is what I have. And the sun still falls on it,
and I still polish it, when I remember.

# The Snug

Confessions held by a stained-glass door,
coloured by tales of affairs and debts,
horses and deaths. So much hanging
in the air, like smoke exhaled in the O
of conversation – of what might have been.
There's something I'm meant not to know.
And maybe, just maybe, if you could share
a little of what goes on behind that clever exterior,
all those smiles and kisses, if you could tell me
about your men, I think I could be happy
with you, could sit and tell what I haven't told
a soul, on this three- four- five-beer evening.
I check the barman isn't by the hatch,
so we can be almost safe – almost sacred.
The beer's foam eases the jaws, allows the teeth
their glory. We keep on, order another,
money on the hatch – a glimpse of the hand,
the wedding ring. The grouse in the snug's glass
turns its head as if to try not to hear
what men do. The hatch flap down, we go back
to ourselves, our common theatre, as if to sup
in silence would be a failure, somehow.

# How Religion Works

I'd had six or seven glasses of fino
fewer tapas
I was seduced
by a thousand candles wrapped in purple
calling from a makeshift table
that light in unison
Catholicism really nails it on colour
I remember you saying that once
as if from a distance

Here was the painful-looking Jesus
his mother's triangular tears
their purple cloaks
I almost bought a candle
told myself it was for Mum
She'd have liked to glitter there with the rest
I was moved
more than I'm comfortable expressing

I watched beyond the steady flicker
the queue slowing
the tableau of women
in tweeds and furs
bending to kiss the crucified foot
Some bent as if they meant to
lick the blood
others clutched the purple robe
reluctant to move on
Here were the believers

No one would've called me out
of that haze of purple
But I wasn't ready
for the communality of that kiss
the whole of Santa Cruz
one mouth after another

# Taking Off Billy Collins's Clothes

It will be morning.
I will ask him to place his second cup
of espresso back in its saucer
as quietly as I know he can
and rise from the typewriter.
I will lead him to another window
where it will be snowing –
this and the horses distract him
while I ease off his jacket,
pull his lemon cashmere sweater over his head.
He will scarcely notice while he listens
for the sound snow makes, slipping away
to a reverie of landscapes he's yet to visit.
As I unbutton his jeans,
his coffee breath
blurs the glass momentarily.
I cannot tell you everything
but he kicks away the crumpled denim
as if shrugging off something half-remembered
and I feel that he's stopped himself
from murmuring something wry,
sensing I may prefer silence.

# The Only Truly Memorable
# New Year's Eve

was the one I spent alone, my image taken
again and again as I leant from the window,
woken by midnight's bells and screams. I watched

the celebrations, all the colours in the sky,
like a little war above South London. And the man
who used to own the sauna snapping away

across the street. Who was lonelier that night –
me struggling out of bed, wanting
to be a part of something, even from afar,

or the man opposite, capturing a woman,
her face flu-white and unwashed, her coral
dressing gown the only interest in the frame?

Unprepared for how bad the New Year would be,
I cursed that neighbour, tried to shout
but no voice came. It's as if the telephoto lens

deflected all my silent *fuck you*'s back
through the open window; so little I could change
and the New Year busy defining itself.

# Elsewhere

When light prods
at the curtain      you look up
having been away
to a place where the news
did not exist
and the journey was calm
for these waters
                    Yet you
sense you've not travelled
enough      wish you'd tipped
over the horizon      known something
of the bend in the world

# Boasting Sonnet

I'm not one to brag but Sharon Olds wrote
me a poem; *me* from a council estate.

I've done handstands, on a skateboard, downhill
yet failed both Maths and English O level.

I'm still in love with the man I met at
eighteen. I don't believe in marriage but

I once won an award for headbanging
and chaired human rights talks at the UN.

Expelled from school, I'm now a PhD.
I don't wear make-up, this is the real me

unless I'm doing panto, in Cornish.
I'm a qualified mountain leader. Wish

you could see my scything *and* lindyhop.
I'd say much more but sonnets make you stop.

# The Smiling of Children
# While They Sleep

*for Ian Duhig*

The Cornish have a word, vestry, for
the smiling of children while they sleep.
As a child, I was known to talk
while I stumbled to school at 3 am
in full uniform, tie knotted. Other nights,
I'd wake my sister when I pirouetted
in pale blue leotard, opaque white tights,
eyes shut. I can't know if I was smiling.
Now my eyes are fully opened; I'm not
a sleeping child. Still, I could smile more.
We all could. Might we all vestry
when a friend dreams of us, or a relative
in another part of the world thinks kindly
of us? And had I had a child, would she be
less troubled than I was? I imagine her
learning *vestry*, facial muscles flexing
on the 'e' and the 'y' – so much more
enjoyable than a cold, mumbled prayer.
A shame this word's no longer on our lips.
Smiling might help: these are difficult times.

# This Isn't a Yellow Cake

*translated from Yohanna Jaramillo's original*

These aren't the six thousand or three point two million years
in the radiocarbon calibration curve,
it's not as if they were Neanderthals or Africans,
it's not as if a third race or a fourth has been created
from the same Universe
and definitely from the same substance.
It matters if we ate each other,
if some of us bled,
if we were naked,
if buildings fell on us.
I embrace all decisions,
all those historical facts,
even Feynman★.
We all went down,
we all went down in a literal sense,
maybe we will all float
on a surfboard,
on the earth's crust.
Between the void
and the void is not a natural number
created to find the route to the matrix (S).
As the young Leyva said: *all realities exist.*


I accept all beliefs,
Lucy and my ancestors' imaginary friends, such as Eve,
are welcome.
Atapuerca and all the tunnels under the sea
are welcome.
The soldiers who return to see their children,
and their adopted pets,
are welcome.
The Panama Canal, Disney, part of Chiapas and all the recreations
    of the world,
are welcome.
But Oxxo and McDonald's
are not welcome.
Medicines, toothpastes, deodorants
are not welcome.

45

Coca Cola, ICE that can't be swallowed, heads of state
are not welcome.
Discoveries made by a fragile mind
do us little good.
Oh children of Coltán!
Oh children of Chernobyl!
Oh children of Rome!
Oh children of the lower case!
When they play hide and seek with 'God',
he gets lost.
Before they find him, he drops Uranium gas
and destroys them.

* *Richard Philips Feynman,*
  *(New York, 1918 – Los Angeles, 1988) US physicist.*

# The Beach Couldn't be Found

under the scorched weed and rubbish, the crows,
the human shit they fed on. The water was so far out,

nothing you'd swim in. Only the dogs sunbathed,
their fleas popping in the heat like corn.

The sea was no colour and there was no path
through the broken things, flies wafting up

and resettling. There could be no way through for us.
The beach didn't know it was a beach,

didn't know what was expected, that it had duties
to perform. No one had told it and it hadn't asked.

The beach was just a place where the land finished.
We were as welcome and as unwelcome as anyone.

# I Saw Them Making Love

on a cobbled side street
only it didn't seem like love.
He was tiny; she was tall
and furious. I walked on,
quickly. I couldn't help
but think of seaside postcards;
men with small penises,
women with huge breasts.
But this was real, a woman
in a party dress, hair up;
the man naked but for a red hat.
You can't not notice something
like that. Neither of them saw me.
He went thrusting on and on
and on. She leant against
the club's wall, looking as if this
were happening to someone else.

# What I Will Tell my Daughter

I will tell my daughter that I'm sorry
I didn't have time for her –
no time to allow her to grow
inside and no time to push her out.
I will tell my daughter I'm sorry
I never wanted her – or her brother –
although, I'll admit, I was curious
as to their personalities, their looks
but not curious enough. I will tell her
I'm sorry I told the man
who would have been her father
that I didn't want her,
that she was better off born to someone else,
that I'm sorry I wasn't prepared
to have her occupy my body,
that I liked the life I had.
I will tell her I didn't want
to share my life with her or share the man
who would have been her father,
that I'm sorry in public but not in private.
I will tell her I didn't have the money
to give her all the things I didn't have –
but that's not the real reason.
I will tell my daughter that I'm sorry
she wasn't wanted or needed or loved.
And she will look into my eyes and tell me
she's long since stopped listening.

# The Reveal

She pulls up her jumper
and it's hard not to look.

At first, I thought, a flesh-coloured bra
– underwired –

but the two half-moons
I'd taken as structure, were scars.

She hugs me, her tough body
like a barrel, nothing like a child's;

titless as she is, the female is there
no matter what's been taken from her,

what's been scooped away.
The scars are so much shinier

than my mum's – who did not survive.
And this woman lives

to pass on her hurt. It's too much for me –
*here, you have it.*

She lifts her jumper again,
a sense of power for her in this celebration

of damage, as if passing on
trauma could somehow lessen hers.

# Three Horses

This horse's skin opens
like a dinner jacket.
I'd show the horse my scars –

my neck and breast,
but we're not alone.
And I'm scared of horses.

This horse is riderless.
I can't help
my gaze falling

on the flaccid penis –
all those clean, gentle folds.
This is not a Stubbs.

I don't like Stubbs's horses.
I'm not frightened of scars.
A horse doesn't respond

to the young boy
who waves and says,
*Goodbye Horse*. At his age,

I was frightened when a rider
reared her horse over me –
all those hooves and unluck.

I'd said the horse was beautiful –
it was deep brown, eyes
as reckless as mine.

# It Was Nothing to Do with Any of You

So many of you asked what I was wearing;
even my best friend asked
what time of night it was,
what I'd been doing.

Yes, I had had a drink.
Several.
And no, I hadn't talked to him,
hadn't *led him on*.

You were only seeking to protect yourselves,
that it couldn't happen to you.
You'd never have been out,
alone, after midnight, cycling
back from Birchington carnival, from the pub,
in a man's vest, no bra, dungarees.
I understand you did this,
so that violence wouldn't come your way.

The same for the drivers who mounted
the grass verge, to avoid the happening
on the inside lane, two bicycles on top
of each other, a woman and a man grappling,
a man on top of a woman.

I was angry at you.
All of you. Angry at my step-father
for leaping out of bed, determined to find
this man, to beat him up –
as if my step-father, too, had been wronged.

It was nothing to do with any of you.

You might just have asked how I was.

# Circling in Flippers

*after Adrienne Rich*

Something of mythology clinging
to me like so much black rubber
but it is me who dives from the blue-green
that intake of sunlight
into the deeper blue    becoming midnight
there are no fish    no one else
no one can follow me here
and he doesn't swim in these waters
can't enter the depths with me
again
           He knows I'd finish the job I started
I've practised on the beach holding
three minutes of air
while others swim and play
                   I dolphin down
to the extent of my lungs
find one leg
of the teak bench embedded in the ocean floor
some of its slats are missing    others trail weed
I would chisel my name into the bench
another form of remembrance
as if I could forget
          He is held
someplace else
a shark cage
diver's knife still strapped to his thigh

# If I Were a Different Person
# I Might be Able to Forgive

He'll be in his 50s
now. Will he be less angry
at others and himself? Does he still
cycle around seaside towns?
Does he carry a knife? If he were
to pedal past, I'd like to think
there'd be no recognition. He'd be fatter,
would've lost his blond spikes,
be uglier, for a man can't do
what he did to so many women and stay
attractive. Even a mirror
would call him out. I pity him.
What made him believe
he could only take what he wanted,
that it would never be given?
You share something with such a person,
those few minutes. Let us imagine
that he has regrets. I don't mark the date
or year, though I know the latter.
I'd like to forgive but can never forget
how I focused on his gelled hair,
not his eyes, his clothes, his hands,
his body – not on what he was doing –
                    but *then* I had to come alive.

# The Blade

just sharpened on the lozenge of whetstone,
did what blades do. I'd bent to the frogs, failed
to scoop one up on my stiff, padded glove. Yet here,
with its eyes half-closed, eyes curving back into its imagination,
right leg extended in all of its gleam, seeming like rubber
or plastic, the frog found nothing but air as it lay

scythed on the soft rush and purple moor grass, the frog's
topside looking back at me — the leg and head
convulsing, then settling, the lower organs rearranged
unmendably and below that half-life, the whiff of something
butcher-fresh would stay with me. And my features
in the blade's trajectory, almost innocent.

# She'd Feel Differently

if he were having sex with a woman.
And however wrong
that sounds, she says it's the truth.
She tells me she's imagined
but done nothing other than kiss
another woman, mouths open, slick with lager.
She's looked but rarely wanted. Whoever
the other man is, she tells me she asks her husband
to brush his teeth, to keep himself safe.
For now, she doesn't want to know.
This makes no sense –
but then sex seldom does. And yes,
I've seen how he looks at men.
For now, she asks that he wipes
the man's scent from his neck.
Eventually, she says, she'll have him choose.

# Not Really About Snow

It lay there, somewhere between Paddington
and home. My yellow suitcase and I
travelled. I listened to Alice Oswald,
Sasha Dugdale, Sean O'Brien, their certain,
warmed voices, floating
from left ear to right, all that machinery
between. The voices found their frequencies
through the flurries. Each spoke – privately, it seemed –
of a long-dead poet, one I'd never truly met
on the page. I stared out into the dark, knowing
the snow was present only at stations.
It seemed to huddle there, in half-illumination,
as if waiting to board. Between times,
there was my profile, listening, and those earrings
 – lobes glowing with red plastic roses –
which didn't quite match my cardy.
There was no one to notice; the carriage as quiet as snow
falling upwards. A reflection is never what a person looks like.
A podcast captures an echo of a person's knowledge.
Yet that night, alone in the empty carriage
but for the voices and for Keats, journeying
for seven hours, I knew my luck. I had a tray
of sushi, the chopsticks crossing themselves,
ginger beer. I felt enchanted with ideas,
neurons sparking towards each other. The carriage
was almost cosy, yesterday's clothes –
their acridity – contained in the case
at my feet, London still wrapped around its wheels.
The drifts of snow out there condensing
like memory before it washes out. But for now,
I had everything. I knew my lover
would be waiting for me on the platform.
I had a home to go to. And I felt blessed.

# Hello Wilhemina

*after Wilhemina Barns-Graham*

You big child
                  still in love
        in your nineties
              with colour

your vermilion anger
                  thrown from wall to wall
        a harsh sound
              against the tones of white

This canvas sears
                  the backs of my eyes
        scars
              with certain light

Yours is a fizzing
                  heat
        for this is serious
              play

Someone told me
                  *Art is quiet*
        He hadn't held his ear
              to your squawk of paint

You brought the outdoors in
                  smeared it flat – the folk of blackbirds
        the squabble of buds –
              the many colours of push

I'm trying to find you, Wilhemina
                  you with the grand name
        for I, too, am scared
              of the dark

You've left me
                nothing but your noise
        a streak of paint
                in the direction of travel

north-east to south-west
                yet if I really listen, Wilhemina
        you've left me this:
                colours chanting their own revolution
                        There is too much white in our lives

# Dent-de-Lion: Our First Farm

Our only farm, with its wheat and cows and kids with red hair.
This was their land, their house and we walked
through the yard where they played, we who knew nothing
of wheat and cows but liked to look, hoping their dog
would be leashed. We walked on the path with wheat
beckoning, and all that sky, and the lane and the cowshed.
We tried to understand something of the land; for we
were sea people; we divide like that. We understood the sea,
its obvious seasons. The machinery and animals and plants
were new. But we went and stood, and looked. We felt glad
of the sight of the sky; even liked the dung's stinking pile,
heaving with flies, as we dared each other to stand near it.
Last time we walked there, this was as far
as you could go, as if you were my tiny sister again.
The manure still hazed on the path; the red-haired children,
the dog, the cows, all gone; just the one rotting green tractor.
But the wheat still called and the sky felt huge; unending

# You Can't Know of This

*for Melissa*

I take this morning's walk for you
I go calmly     clearing each fallen branch

from the path     heave it into the river below
as if you were walking behind me

We're 300 miles apart     no phone     no email
Today you get your results

My letter     with its hesitant     frail words
is driving towards you

All I can do is clear the path
as if you will walk here

when you're better     I wait
by the river for a flash of turquoise

I'm out of luck     I've sent it all to you
Whatever happens     the river will keep thundering

I leave a few twigs on the path
for just the minor things to trouble you

# Talisman

She's meant to be good
with words, used to medicating others
with a timely postcard – FABULOUS WOMAN YOU!
Today she can't find it in herself to buy,
let alone send, A SISTER IS WORTH A THOUSAND FRIENDS.
If only she knew the right phrase,
the sort other people have stored in their mouths,
like a kindly tongue.
                       Cards as commands,
white and black shouts on a carousel,
IT'S CHOCOLATE O'CLOCK!
The shopkeeper can't find it in herself
to say *good morning*, even in lower case,
as she heaves her cleavage about by the till.
Maybe these cards aren't even meant
for other people, just something to tack above your screen
YOU MAKE ME PROUD or I LOVE MYSELF
instead of explaining, in another language,
what you think of your boss,
his love of himself.
                     She still doesn't know what to send,
what to say, as if sweet-sweet words on an angel,
LOVE on a butterfly or a pale heart from China
could keep her sister from harm.

# My Sister and the Heavy Magic

I have watched her walk into the nuclear zone,
fix a needle to the back of her hand, swallow
a clutch of pink pills. The cancer thought

it was safe with her breast, one that would nurture
and support, as if it had just been born –
a rotten baby, sucking at all the goodness,

clawing on with its little nails. It had not expected her
to maim and torture, to limit its tricks
with so much heavy magic. By now it had hoped

to be free of the breast, to have travelled elsewhere,
like a holiday – somewhere to swim and procreate.
The cancer has been poisoned, scraped out,

burned. My sister wraps and coils her head
in roses and birds, as if in celebration,
staggers through her days. Her nights slowly lengthen.

# All Those Years

you had a photo of me and my sister
tiny girls     in a satin frame     whose colour was no longer true
Is that how you thought of us     if you did think of us
in your orchard in Sussex     all those years nursing in the States
The things I've learnt from one phone call
My sister found you
survived by your new wife of 40 years     My sister
tells me   you seemed kind     a lover of wildlife     a carer     making up
perhaps     for your brief time with us
It's hard to know you     I know
what I knew aged seven     My sister says she'll visit your new wife
again     walk in the orchard you planted     stroke your dogs
I will stay out of the picture     hold on to what I knew of you
how you lied     had your affairs     refused maintenance
Still     I'm touched by that mention
of a well-travelled satin frame     red     possibly Chinese
And if I think of you     I think of a side parting     cravat     pipe
country check shirt     a pint of bitter
I hear you were playing
with one of your dogs     threw a ball     fell in the orchard
At the age of seven     I sent you away
no longer prepared to visit     You never tried to change
my mind     didn't write or call
I sense you at the back of my jaws
when I'm trying not to cry     A nurse all your life I hear
a footballer     with a house full of books     All those things
I can't now unknow
My sister says she'll show me your photo
It's easy to be kind to the dead     If I could keep my life tidy     I would

# The Sun & Me

How sad I was when the man with the pretty mouth said
you were dying     That this won't happen for 5 billion years

didn't make so much difference     Your glorious fizz
like a giant orange bath bomb     is waning

your supply of nuclear fuel in flux     You're midway
through your life cycle     like me     We're both warming up

My hypothalamus is going awry     as oestrogen shrivels
You have your own ageing process     a lack of hydrogen

If I could     I'd fly to you     the largest canister of H
in the universe     flush to my back     I want to help

replenish the only form of nuclear fusion I can support
You're so far from me     yet you're a reminder

we won't always be here     Your helium speeds the sound
orbiting my mouth     *You are dying*

I have my own weather these days     a sudden vasodilation
my own climate change     as if you are inside     your rays

radiating through my core     My body soaks the sheets
I spend afternoons in special undies waiting for you

I sprawl all the better to receive you     I know I need protection
I bathe all the same     I like to think

solar flares are you reaching out to me     a kind of magnetism
Perhaps you don't understand how flammable I am

I sense we could never be friends     You will always look down on me
Yet you're not so far from me on the periodic table

I've fewer years remaining     and so much to achieve
I listen for your voice     your pitch too high for human ears

I wear my glasses to see you better     witness
your heaty trajectory     your dive into the sea each night

as if you too     like any menopausal woman
are doing your best to cool down

# The Future Ends Soon

*Montol is the celebration of the wonderful, anarchic and colourful traditions of the Midwinter here in Cornwall, and Cornwall is a better place for it* – Simon Reed

We're drinking brandy after Montol, a night of dancing
outdoors, our masks lit up with LEDs.
Now, there's just three of us
making the longest night a little shorter.
Ella toasts: *To the New Year.*

Something drops,
like all the needles from an evergreen
and I understand, in the way I understood
that the border between Scotland and England
had been shifted north, ignoring the obvious
wall, how natural this was as a boundary.
I understand that something's diminished
– not just a nation's domain –
but there's the replacement of what already exists:
a wall, the sun, the moon, the days lengthening.
Of course, this solstice shift, this is New Year.

I feel both stupid and enlightened,
a sense of wonder about my new friends
and Kernow, and the brandy I never thought I liked;
I congratulate myself on my choice of companions
knowing something's shifted: not just the realisation
that ancient knowledge has been quashed
and replaced by the dull, the numbered;
there are other beliefs, those you find half-way
down a bottle of brandy; some are for keeps,
like your new date for New Year, your newfound love
of all things cognac, and the people who teach you –
the ones who've lived here, in this place, forever.

# Transistor

With the garble of electricity came a whisper of love.
Tuning the dial's bronze ridge with glossy nails

ushered in new saints, whose urgent message
I couldn't quite catch amid the whine and hiss,

the shifting interference of megahertz.
I listened hard, harder than I'd ever listened

to Sister Ferdinand. And here was Vienna,
Hilversum, Lyons, Brussels: sing-song voicewaves

pulsing into the night, when everyone who felt safe
in their thoughts was asleep. I wanted to be told

how to live, wanted guidance from the weak light
of Europe; a mono transmission of hope.

# Yellow Eyes, the Usual Big Teeth

The wolf's on the bridleway above me      moving
in the trees      our paths likely to coincide today
next week      next year      The wolf is always there
but I walk in the oaky woods      like anyone
almost without thinking      or so I kid myself
We will come face to face      mine flatter      his pointier
I can't continue to live for what might be and when
The air's still cool      Some might see an obsession
in my walking      so that no more is taken
than what's already been taken      The sun pushes up
like a wild flower      lime-greening everything
I smell magpies      hear the huge bumblebee wings
of a pheasant      but they      like the wolf      remain unseen
Bluebells curl like ferns      their blue not as devastating
as I'd hoped for      I know the glitter of yellow eyes
my mind talks into its old patterns      Everything's crooked
on this path      Eight sleeping cows in a field
lie like dollops of yoghurt      I breathe in
their easy sleep      forgetting the wolf
for the time it takes for a cloud to pass      I step
back      cross the slab of granite
There's wolves wherever you go

# The Guns

I was once given this advice:
*If you write about a gun, it has to go off.*
Well, that's not going to happen
here; there are some things I can control.
I told the man I wasn't impressed
when he unwrapped an ordinary duster –
you know, the fluffy yellow kind –
and there was a dark, almost Bakelite shape
something toy about it, and squat –
a toad is more attractive – and the barrel
clunkier than I'd have thought.
It brought its own silence.
I half-expected a gun to have allure
in the way of a cigarette placed
between lips, and lit. I hadn't asked
to see this, hadn't known what he would
unwrap. I focused on the contrast
between yellow and black; how he'd chosen
danger colours, subconsciously.
Later, I wondered why he felt the need
for a gun. He was gentle with it
admired it as you might a kitten
cradled in his lap. I told him to put it away
as I would if he'd shown me his penis.
He'd hoped for a reaction, something
to make his freckled skin harder, impermeable.
I didn't taste threat, or fear, at the time.
Since then, I've had a gun pointed at me –
when I jumped off the train at the border
of Hungary, in the wrong place –
there was a lot of shouting. I got back on.
And again, on a farm, where I strayed
from the path; and once more, on a moor
where a ghillie shouldn't have been doing
what he was. He studied me
along the length of a horse-brown shotgun.
No woman I've encountered has unwrapped
her gun or pointed it at me, or allowed a gun
to speak for or show her emotion.
I'm not quite sure what this says.
I know not everything is in my control.

# Acknowledgements

Thanks to the editors of the following, where some of these poems first appeared: Arnolfini website; *B O D Y*; *The Compass*; *The Dark Horse*; *The Fenland Reed*; *The Fiddlehead*; *Finished Creatures*; #filmvpoetry; *Hwaet! 20 Years of Ledbury Poetry Festival* (Bloodaxe, 2016); *The London Magazine*; *The Manhattan Review*; *The Missouri Review*; *Modern Poetry in Translation*; *Mslexia*; *The New Walk*; *Oxford Poetry*; *Poems in Which*; *Poetry Ireland Review*; *Poetry London*; *The Poetry Review*; *Poetry Wales*; *Project Boast* (Triarchy Press, 2018); *Raceme*; *The Spectator*; *Truths* (TellTale Press, 2018); *Typhoon Etiquette* (Verve Poetry Press, 2019); *Wild Court*; *Witches, Warriors and Workers* (ed. Fran Lock, Culture Matters, 2020).

I'm grateful to the following residencies, which have sparked ideas for many of these poems: Arnolfini, Brisons Veor, Hawthornden International Writer's Retreat, Leach Pottery, Lorna and Roger Farnworth Residency (with thanks to David Woolley and Ann Gray), and to Hils Tranter for loaning The Barns.

I'm also grateful to Judy Brown for The Conversation, a letter-based collaboration, which has prompted several of these poems.

'Anti- ambient' and 'London: A Reply' appeared in #filmvpoetry, an online project with the visual artist Tim Ridley.

'Spared' and 'Three Horses' were written during a residency at the Arnolfini, in response to Daphne Wright's show 'Emotional Archeology'.

'The Only Truly Memorable New Year's Eve' and 'The Reveal' were nominated for The Best of the Net 2017.

'Boasting Sonnet' was commissioned by Alyson Hallett and Rachel Bentham for Project Boast.

'Dualism: A Manifesto' was commissioned for SolForce, a 'rampant solstice celebration', organised by the artist Jesse Leroy Smith, to raise money for Freedom from Torture.

'Interpretation' and 'What Arrival Feels Like' were published in *Typhoon Etiquette*, Verve Poetry Press, 2019.

Yohanna Jaramillo is a Mexican poet. Her latest collection is *El Valle*, Editorial Domingo Atrasado, 2019. For more on her poetry, see www.yohannajaramillo.blogspot.com.

Steve Penhaligon is a bard of the Cornish Gorsedh and runs a Cornish language class in Heamoor.

Thank you to everyone who commented on these poems, including members of Falmouth Poetry Group and Penzance Stanza. Particular thanks to Sarah Barnsley, Judy Brown and Penelope Shuttle, to my editor Amy Wack, and to the team at Seren.

Thank you to Liz Berry, Malika Booker and Helen Mort.

With thanks to Arts Council England/British Council for an International Artists' Development Grant, to Maura Dooley at Goldsmiths and to Michiyo Takano at Yamanashi Prefectural University.

Finally, heartfelt thanks to the Society of Authors for an Authors' Foundation Grant, which enabled me to complete this collection.